PREDATORS

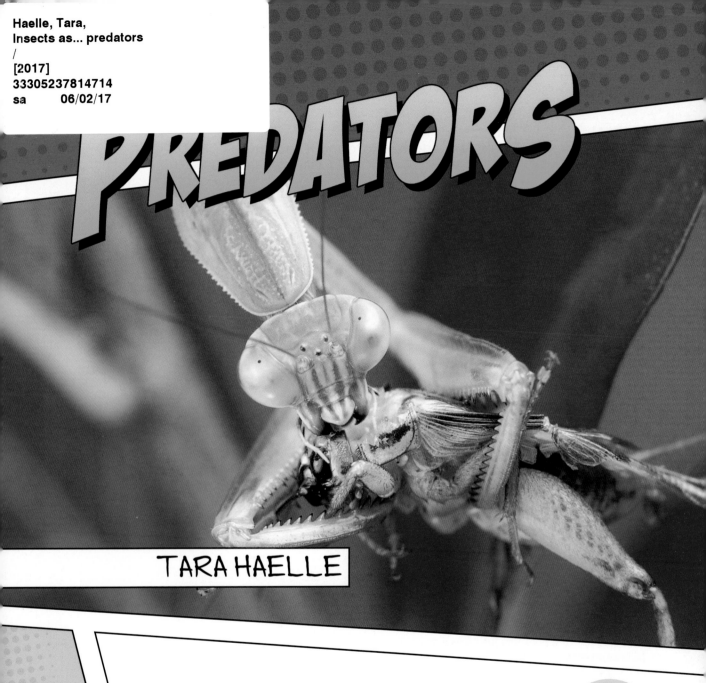

TARA HAELLE

Rourke
Educational Media

rourkeeducationalmedia.com

Scan for Related Titles
and Teacher Resources

Before Reading:

Building Academic Vocabulary and Background Knowledge

Before reading a book, it is important to tap into what your child or students already know about the topic. This will help them develop their vocabulary, increase their reading comprehension, and make connections across the curriculum.

1. *Look at the cover of the book. What will this book be about?*
2. *What do you already know about the topic?*
3. *Let's study the Table of Contents. What will you learn about in the book's chapters?*
4. *What would you like to learn about this topic? Do you think you might learn about it from this book? Why or why not?*
5. *Use a reading journal to write about your knowledge of this topic. Record what you already know about the topic and what you hope to learn about the topic.*
6. *Read the book.*
7. *In your reading journal, record what you learned about the topic and your response to the book.*
8. *After reading the book complete the activities below.*

Content Area Vocabulary
Use glossary words in a sentence.

abdomen
camouflage
ecosystem
larvae
mandibles
pests
predators
prey
reproduce
venom

After Reading:

Comprehension and Extension Activity

After reading the book, work on the following questions with your child or students in order to check their level of reading comprehension and content mastery.

1. *What would happen if we didn't have insect predators in the ecosystem? (Summarize)*
2. *Name an interesting fact about the black whirligig beetle. (Infer)*
3. *What is a favorite treat for firefly larvae? (Asking questions)*
4. *How long can the giant water bug grow to be? (Text to self connection)*
5. *What is one of the bulldog ants secret weapons for attacking its prey? (Asking questions)*

Extension Activity

Insect predators! In the book you read about some pretty interesting insects and the ways they sting or kill their prey. Pick your favorite insect from the book. Do some further research on the Internet and learn all you can about it. Now, write a research paper including all your findings. Share it with your class.

TABLE OF CONTENTS

PREDATORS IN THE GARDEN

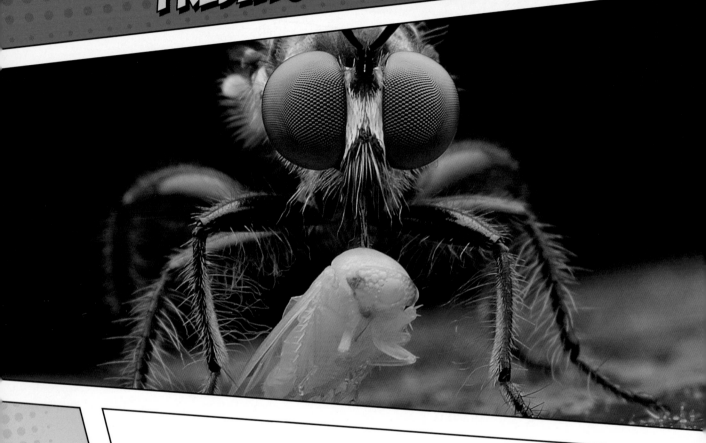

What are the most ferocious animal hunters you can think of? Tigers? Wolverines? Grizzly bears? Sharks? What about critters that fit in the palm of your hand? Many insects are powerful hunters too. Insects that eat other animals are **predators**. The creatures they eat are their **prey**.

Insect predators may eat other insects or larger animals, including spiders, fish, reptiles, mammals, and birds. Some insects are only predators as **larvae**. Larvae are the immature insects that hatch from eggs. As adults, they may eat only plants or dead animals.

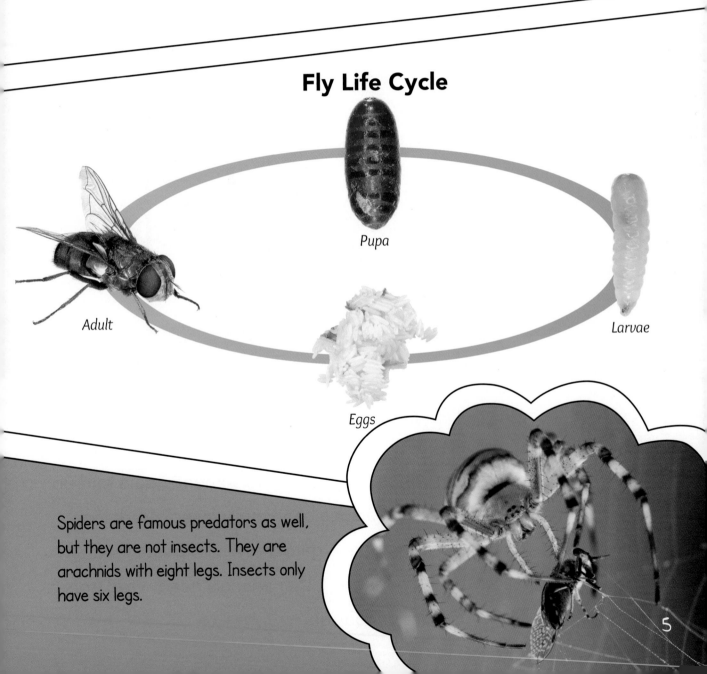

Fly Life Cycle

Pupa

Larvae

Adult

Eggs

Spiders are famous predators as well, but they are not insects. They are arachnids with eight legs. Insects only have six legs.

Predators play an important part in the **ecosystem**. Without them, too many other insects or other animals would **reproduce**. Then the environment would end up with an unequal balance of animals. Insect predators are especially helpful in gardens. Insect **pests** feed on plants that humans and other animals need. Predators keep pests under control.

Ladybugs are expert garden predators. Their favorite meal is aphids. Aphids are tiny green insects that munch leaves. The more ladybugs that live in a garden, the healthier those plants often are.

Insect predators live in every imaginable climate. Ice crawlers, called grylloblattids, prefer frigid climates where they prey on dying or dead insects.

7

Green lacewing larvae also chomp on aphids and other pests. These larvae spend several weeks filling up on aphids, spider mites, thrips, mealybugs, caterpillars, and beetle larvae. Then the lacewing larvae spin a cocoon. They emerge as adults two weeks later and only eat nectar, honeydew, and flower pollen.

Green lacewing larva

Thrip

Slugs and snails also tear up gardens, but they are favorite treats for firefly larvae. Sometimes baby fireflies will even follow a trail of slime to find their prey! They use long, curled mouthparts to inject a chemical into it. This chemical paralyzes the prey so the larvae can suck out its insides. Yum!

Firefly larva

Snail

Whoosh! A dragonfly swoops close to the water to grab a mosquito in its jaws in mid-flight. A waterbug waits silently on the surface until it sees a chance to snag a minnow. Streams and ponds are filled with insect predators, in the air and under the water.

10

Dragonflies hover over ponds, rivers, and creeks. These iridescent, big-eyed beauties dart back and forth with two large sets of latticework wings. They catch and consume small insects in mid-air. Even in the water, dragonfly larvae hunt worms, fish, and tadpoles. Damselflies are cousins of dragonflies. Some damselflies in the rainforests of Central and South America even feed on spiders.

Dragonflies wings are iridescent. This means their colors seem to change when you look at them from different angles.

Ancient dragonflies were possibly the largest insects ever to live on Earth. With wingspans wider than two feet (.6 meters) and bodies up to 17 inches (.43 meters), they were as big as seagulls!

Dozens of insects skate, walk, or float like boats on the water's surface. Water-measurers cautiously prowl atop the water, looking for tiny insects and animals to spear with its mouthpart.

Black whirligig beetles swirl in circles around each other. They have one pair of eyes below the water's surface and one pair above. These scavengers pounce on any insect they can find.

Long-legged, slender water striders hunt while skating across ponds, lakes, and even oceans. They are nicknamed "Jesus bugs" because they walk on water and don't get wet.

Water tiger

Diving beetles are so fierce they will dive after prey much bigger than them. They catch fish, frogs, toads, salamanders, tadpoles, and other insects in their forceful jaws. Their equally vicious larvae are called water tigers.

Watch out for the backswimmers. They bite people too! They coast under the surface on boat-shaped backs. An air bubble on their **abdomen** lets them breathe. When a fish, insect, or tadpole swims close enough, they lunge and bite. Their saliva dissolves the prey's insides so it can slurp them out.

The giant water bug has a pair of pincers and a beak for injesting digestive enzymes into its victim.

The most powerful pond predator is the giant water bug. They can grow to 4 inches (10 centimeters) long. That's bigger than your hand! They paddle with their four back legs and catch fish, frogs, salamanders, snakes, and even turtles with their mighty front legs.

ANTS & WASPS & FLIES, OH MY!

People know to avoid insects like fire ants and wasps because of their painful stings. But that sting is nothing compared to being on the menu of these predators.

Most bees dine on nectar and pollen, but not Japanese hornets. These hornets capture any insect they can—even honeybees—and tear it apart to feed their larvae.

17

Fire ants will eat just about anything, plant or animal, dead or alive. They gobble up eggs of spiders, cockroaches, and butterflies. The paralyzing **venom** in their stingers can kill animals a thousand times bigger than them. These tiny terrors keep biting to take down scorpions, grasshoppers, caterpillars, toads, songbirds, lizards, snakes, and even newborn mice and chicks!

Massive bulldog ants in Australia are just as fierce. They are one inch (2.5 centimeters) long with powerful jaws for grasping prey. They curl up their abdomen to sting their victim several times.

Trap-jaw ants have the fastest jaws on the planet—2,300 times faster than the blink of an eye! They use their jaws to seize prey. They also use them to launch themselves high in the air.

19

Red velvet ants look like ants but are actually wasps. They have a sting so painful they're nicknamed "cow killers." But it's the juveniles who are predators of other wasps and bees. One of their prey is also a predator: the cicada killer wasp.

These wasps paralyze big cicadas and drag them to an underground **burrow**. Then the wasp lays an egg on the trapped cicada. It becomes food for the wasp's larvae. But when the larvae build their cocoons, the velvet ant lays its eggs on the cocoon. The velvet ant larvae then feed on the wasp larvae.

Some flies are predators too. Scorpionflies only sometimes eat insects, but their cousins, hangingflies, are sneaky hunters. They hang and wait for mosquitos, flies, and moths they can capture with their clawed legs.

Hangingfly

Dance flies only hunt for mating. Males capture an insect and wrap it in silk like a present. Then they dance together with their gifts until a female chooses one of them. He gives her the wrapped insect, and the feast gives her enough protein to grow eggs.

Dance flies are known for their mating swarms, which sometimes occur during daylight, but most often at dusk when they are very difficult to see.

CLEVER HUNTING STRATEGIES

Predator insects capture prey in creative ways. Robber flies and praying mantises are stealthy waiters. Robber flies perch on stems and use their excellent eyesight to wait for a beetle, a grasshopper, or wasp to come by. With incredible speed, robber flies snatch their prey mid-air and inject venom. The venom digests the prey so the flies can suck out the insides.

Praying mantises look like leaves or stems. They stay perfectly still, and their **camouflage** helps them hide. When a tasty treat comes near, they use sharp hooks on their forelegs to grab prey in a split second. They dine on insects, spiders, lizards, birds, and even snakes.

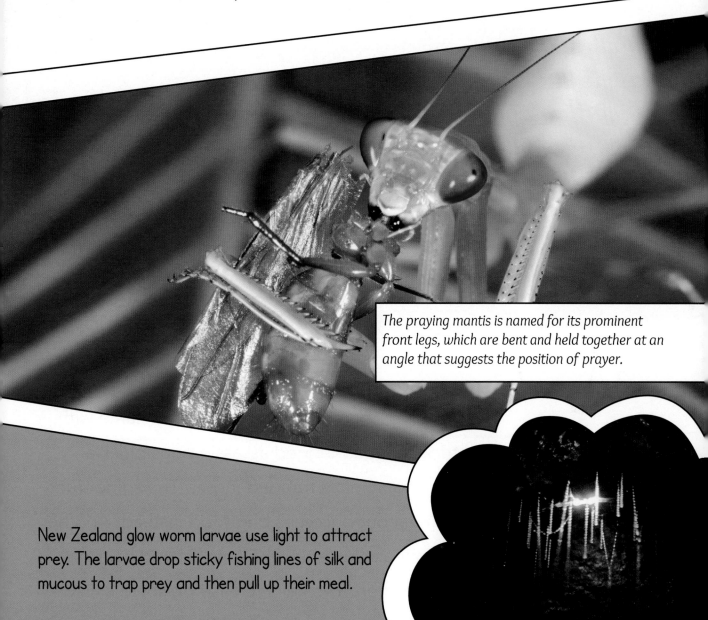

The praying mantis is named for its prominent front legs, which are bent and held together at an angle that suggests the position of prayer.

New Zealand glow worm larvae use light to attract prey. The larvae drop sticky fishing lines of silk and mucous to trap prey and then pull up their meal.

Assassin bugs live up to their murderous name with several tricks. Thread-legged assassin bugs pluck a spider's web to mimic a trapped insect. The spider runs out for its meal but becomes bug food instead! Another assassin bug feasts on ants. The ants lick red hairs on the bug's abdomen. The hairs release poisonous fluid that paralyzes the ants.

Tiger beetles use their speed to chase down prey by land or air. For their size, these ferocious beetles run faster than any other animal in the world. A human as fast as a tiger beetle would run over 300 miles (483 kilometers) per hour! Their sharp **mandibles** can rip any other insect to pieces.

Antlion larvae dig steep, funnel-shaped sand traps. They wait at the bottom until an insect steps on the edge. It falls down the pit into the antlion larvae's jaws.

27

African ants called siafu find strength in numbers. They are also called army or driver ants because they travel as a huge swarm. They overwhelm and devour anything in their path. Even cows, goats, and other large animals may become their banquet. Siafu are the only ants who might attack and kill a human, but it's very rare.

Army ants are considered one of the deadliest creatures in the world. They hunt in large groups, eating anything that stands in their way, but only if it moves.

Tarantula hawks are huge wasps that pursue even bigger spiders. In a face-to-face battle, a female wasp slides under and flips a tarantula. She stings and paralyzes the spider and then carries it off to a burrow. She lays one egg, and the larva that hatches feeds on the tarantula for weeks.

GLOSSARY

abdomen (AB-duh-muhn): the rear section of an insect's body

camouflage (KAM-uh-flahzh): a disguise or a natural coloring that allows animals, people, or objects to hide by making them look like their surroundings

ecosystem (EE-koh-sis-tuhm): all the living things in a place and their relation to their environment

larvae (LAHR-vee): insects at the stage of development between egg and a pupa, when they look like worms

mandibles (MAN-duh-buhls): the jaws or crushing parts of an insect's mouth

pests (pests): insects or other animals that destroy or damage crops, food, or livestock

predators (PRED-uh-turs): animals that live by hunting other animals for food

prey (pray): an animal that is hunted by another animal for food

reproduce (ree-pruh-DOOS): to produce offspring or individuals of the same kind

venom (VEN-uhm): poison produced by some snakes, spiders, and insects

INDEX

SHOW WHAT YOU KNOW

1. Why are predators important to ecosystems?

2. What kinds of insects use venom to paralyze their prey?

3. What kind of insect uses camouflage to hunt?

4. What kinds of insects are predators mostly as larvae?

5. Name another clever way that insects hunt or capture prey.

WEBSITES TO VISIT

http://kids.sandiegozoo.org/animals/insects

www.biokids.umich.edu/critters/Insecta/

www.ars.usda.gov/is/kids/insects/insectintro.htm

ABOUT THE AUTHOR

Tara Haelle spent much of her youth exploring creeks and forests outside and reading books inside. As an adult, she's traveled across the world on exciting adventures. She earned a photojournalism degree from the University of Texas at Austin so she could keep learning about the world by interviewing scientists and writing about their work. She lives in central Illinois with her husband and two sons. You can learn more about her at her website: www.tarahaelle.net.

www.rourkeeducationalmedia.com

PHOTO CREDITS: Cover © &#169 Cathy Keifer, Christian Musat; Page 1 © Luc Viatour/www.lucnix.be; Page 3 © Nico Smit; Page 4 © rhonny dayusasono; Page 5 © Protasov AN, Lion Hijmans; Page 6 © Cornel Constantin; Page 7 © Joseph Calev, www.opencage.info; Page 8 © Henrik Larsson, Katarina Christenson; Page 9 © Txanbelin; Page 10 © fastfun23; Page 11 © Josef Sowa, 1001nights; Page 12 © Ian Redding; Page 13 © blinkwinkel/Alamy Stock Photo, grafzart8888; Page 14 © Julia Shemenko, Igor Semenov; Page 15 © Jivko Nakev; Page 16 © Aaskolnick; Page 17 © wikipedia, eethercollector; Page 18 © SARIN KUNTHONG; Page 19 © Peter bertok, Kurt_G; Page 20 © exOrzist; Page 21 © Elliote Rusty Harold; Page 22 © Richard Bartz, Cody Hough; Page 23 © Mirko Graul; Page 24 © Padung; Page 25 © Dr. Morley Read, Wikipedia; Page 26 © Jansen Chua; Page 27 © David Parsons, D. Kucharski K. Kucharska; Page 28 © Mehmet Karatay, April Nobile/www.antweb.org; Page 29 © DaveHood

Edited by: Keli Sipperley
Cover design by: Tara Raymo *www.creativelytara.com*
Interior design by: Jen Thomas

Insects as Predators / Tara Haelle
(Insects As …)
ISBN (hard cover)(alk. paper) 978-1-68191-695-8
ISBN (soft cover) 978-1-68191-796-2
ISBN (e-Book) 978-1-68191-894-5
Library of Congress Control Number: 2016932571

Library of Congress PCN Data

Also Available as:

Printed in the United States of America, North Mankato, Minnesota